The Civil War

Researching American History

edited by

Arden Bowers

Facing the enemy, Tennessee, 1862

Discovery Enterprises, Ltd.
Carlisle, Massachusetts

First Edition © Discovery Enterprises, Ltd., Carlisle, MA 2001

ISBN 1-57960-071-9

Library of Congress Catalog Card Number 00-110343

10   9   8   7   6   5   4   3   2   1

Printed in the United States of America

Subject Reference Guide:

Title: *The Civil War*
Series: *Researching American History*
edited by Arden Bowers

Nonfiction
Analyzing documents re: The Civil War

Credits:

Cover illustration: The mess line Union camp, 1863 (Mediasource)

Other illustrations: Mason-Dixon line map, p. 6, *The American Heritage Dictionary of the English Language,* 1970, p. 802

Acknowledgments:

Special thanks to Phyllis Raybin Emert for her research and editing of documents excerpted from *Women in the Civil War,* Copyright, Discovery Enterprises, Ltd., Lowell, MA 1995

and to

Stephen M. Forman, for his research and editing of documents excerpted from *Echoes of the Civil War: The Blue* and *Echoes of the Civil War: The Gray,* Copyright, Discovery Enterprises, Ltd., Carlisle, MA, 1997

The primary source documents in this book rely heavily upon and excerpt their work.

Contents

About the Series

Researching American History is a series of books which introduces various topics and periods in our nation's history through the study of primary source documents.

Reading the Historical Documents

On the following pages you'll find words written by people during or soon after the time of the events. This is firsthand information about what life was like back then. Illustrations are also created to record history. These historical documents are called **primary source materials**.

At first, some things written in earlier times may seem difficult to understand. Language changes over the years, and the objects and activities described might be unfamiliar. Also, spellings were sometimes different. Below is a model which describes how we help with these challenges.

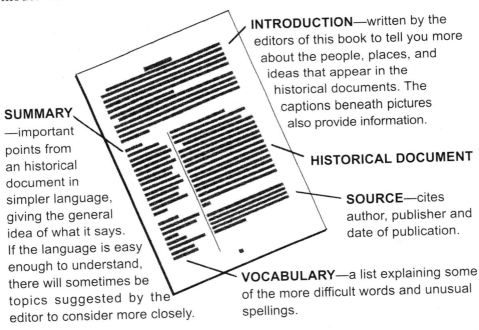

INTRODUCTION—written by the editors of this book to tell you more about the people, places, and ideas that appear in the historical documents. The captions beneath pictures also provide information.

SUMMARY—important points from an historical document in simpler language, giving the general idea of what it says. If the language is easy enough to understand, there will sometimes be topics suggested by the editor to consider more closely.

HISTORICAL DOCUMENT

SOURCE—cites author, publisher and date of publication.

VOCABULARY—a list explaining some of the more difficult words and unusual spellings.

In these historical documents, you may see three periods (...) called an ellipsis. It means that the editor has left out some words or sentences. You may see some words in brackets, such as [and]. These are words the editor has added to make the meaning clearer. When you use a document in a paper you're writing, you should include any ellipses and brackets it contains, just as you see them here. Be sure to give complete information about the author, title, and publisher of anything that was written by someone other than you.

Introduction

by

Arden Bowers

The Civil War, also called "The War between the States," "The War of the Rebellion," and "The War for Southern Independence," began in April 1861, and lasted until late April 1865. It pitted North against South, and sometimes brother against brother, or father against son, in a series of devastating battles and philosophical confrontations that would divide the nation for years after its last official conflict. At the end of the war, the Northern victory brought freedom to four million slaves and began a period of Reconstruction that would continue into the 20th century.

The North and the South had become very different regions during the years before the Civil War began. The South was mostly farmland, including large plantations that grew enormous fields of cotton. Southern farmers needed massive numbers of slaves to work in the fields. The South resisted building factories, preferring to maintain their farms and small-town lives. They also hung onto their love of states' rights, some even referring to their states as their "countries."

The North, on the other hand, contained many factories that did not use slave labor. Northerners had smaller farms, more cities, larger businesses and a more extensive network of roads and railroads than Southerners. Because of growing businesses that served more than one state, Northerners recognized the benefits of all the states being centralized and united under one government.

As new Western states were admitted to the Union, the North and South argued about whether or not each new state should have slaves. Some of the new states were allowed to decide about slavery for themselves, sometimes causing the eruption of small, internal wars over the issue of slavery.

When Abraham Lincoln was elected president in 1860, the South felt that slavery and the southern way of life were severely threatened. Lincoln was steadfastly against slavery and wanted a nation where all the states were united. War was a clear threat as the southern states expressed their anger and supported their beliefs that each state had the right to govern itself.

By the time Lincoln took office in March 1861, seven Southern states had seceded [withdrawn] from the Union and formed their own government, called the Confederacy. Both sides began to recruit volunteers for their armies.

As the two sides planned for battle, the North knew it would have to invade the South and defeat the Confederacy on its own turf, in order to force it to come back into the Union. The South believed it could defend itself long enough for the North to run out of money, fresh soldiers, and supplies. The North realized it would have to squeeze the Southern states by coming down the Mississippi River and separating the Western Confederate states from those east of the river. Union forces would also have to invade the South's eastern shores in order to cut off access to its ports. (Southern ports were vital to the Confederacy because they allowed an influx of supplies from Europe, badly needed for war.)

How the Nation Was Divided
By 1861, there were nineteen free states [states that would not allow slavery] and fifteen slave states. Eleven slave states had seceded from the Union and formed the Confederacy. The territories in the middle of the country remained undecided. Even though there were slave and free states in the West, the major battles took place east of the Mississippi River. A fairly straight line [called the Mason-Dixon Line] separated the North from the South.

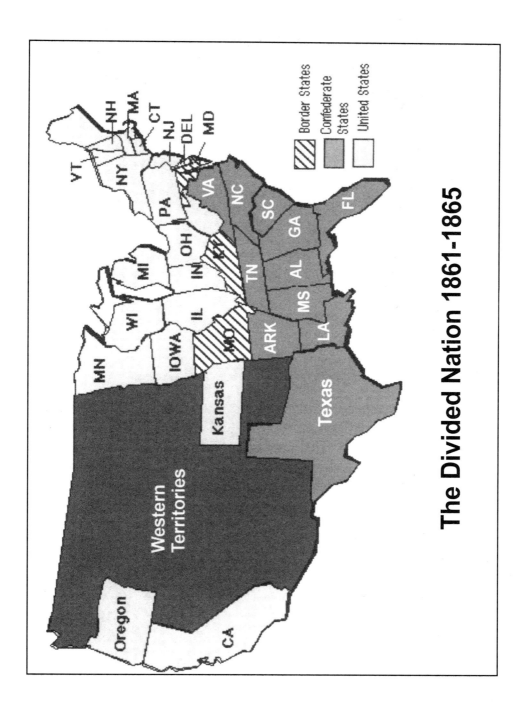

The Divided Nation 1861-1865

Border States

Confederate States

United States

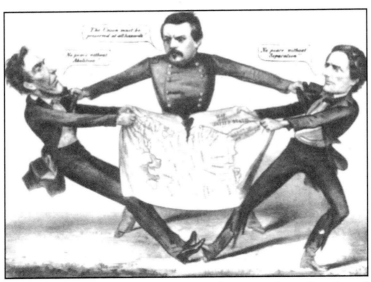

*The North and South aired their differences through political
debates, newspapers, books, and cartoons. This 1864 cartoon
shows Democratic candidate George McClellan trying to keep
the North and South from pulling the nation apart.*

A Nation is Pulled Apart

Bitter fights about slavery tore the American people apart. After Abraham
Lincoln was elected president in 1860, seven Southern states withdrew from
the Union and chose their own president, Jefferson Davis, to lead the Confederacy [the group of states which seceded from the Union].

Slavery

Slavery became a passionate issue as people wrote and spoke about the
cruel treatment of slaves. Many Southerners felt that these descriptions of the
brutal treatment of slaves were not true or, at least, exaggerated. The South
also became more defensive about its right to maintain its way of life.

Harriet Beecher Stowe

In 1852, Harriet Beecher Stowe wrote a popular, antislavery book called *Uncle Tom's Cabin*. The book enraged many people, and contributed to the beginning of the Civil War.

From *Uncle Tom's Cabin*

The child, a boy of ten months, was uncommonly large and strong of his age, and very vigorous in his limbs....

"That's a fine chap!" said a man, suddenly stopping opposite to him, with his hands in his pockets., "How old is he?"

"Ten months and a half," said the mother....

"Rum fellow!" said the man. "Knows what's what!" and he whistled, and walked on. When he had got to the other side of the boat, he came across Haley, who was smoking on top of a pile of boxes....

"Taking her down south?" said the man.

Haley nodded and smoked on....

"They won't want the young 'un on the plantation," said the man.

"I shall sell him, first chance I find," said Haley, lighting another cigar....

"Well, stranger, what will you take?"

"Well now," said Haley, "I could raise that ar chap myself, or get him raised; he's uncommon likely and healthy, and he'd fetch a hundred dollars, six months hence; and, in a year or two, he'd bring two hundred, if I had him in the right spot;—so I shan't take a cent less nor fifty for him now."

Source: Harriet Beecher Stowe, *Uncle Tom's Cabin.* New York: Penguin Books, 1981, pp. 205-6. (Originally published in 1852)

Summary:

The ten-month-old [black] boy was large, strong, and energetic. A man stopped and asked his mother the infant's age. The man commented that he looked like a smart baby, before he walked away. The man then talked with a man named Haley. Haley said he was taking the mother South, to be a slave. They agreed that the baby would not be wanted on the plantation. The man said he would buy the baby for fifty dollars because he knew the child would be worth much more money in a year or two.

Vocabulary:

chap = male

fetch = get

hence = later

limbs = arms and legs

rum fellow = good-looking boy

The South Carolina Declaration

South Carolina was the first state to secede from the Union on December 20, 1860. The following declaration was written to explain this decision.

Summary:
Thousands of slaves have been encouraged to run away or rebel.

The new president [Abraham Lincoln] has said that the Government cannot tolerate half of its states using slaves and the other half wanting to free them. He seems to be saying that all slavery will end.

We, therefore, declare that we consider our state a separate nation. We have the right to wage war, name our own allies, trade with other countries, and act as other independent states do.

Vocabulary:
alliances = friends
emissaries = agents, representatives
extinction = destruction
incited = started, urged
insurrection = revolt
intrusted = given responsibility
levy = raise, enlist for service
rectitude = decency
servile = actions of a servant

They have encouraged and assisted thousands of our slaves to leave their homes; and those who remain, have been incited by emissaries, books, and pictures, to servile insurrection.

...A geographical line has been drawn across the Union, and all of the States north of that line have united in the election of a man to the high office of President of the United States whose opinions and purposes are hostile to Slavery. He is to be intrusted with the administration of the common Government, because he has declared that "Government cannot endure permanently half slave, half free," and that the public mind must rest in the belief that Slavery is in the course of ultimate extinction.

. . . .

We, therefore, the people of South Carolina, by our delegates in Convention assembled, appealing to the Supreme Judge of the world for the rectitude of our intentions, have solemnly declared that the Union heretofore existing between this State and the other States of North America is dissolved and that the State of South Carolina has resumed her position among the nations of the world, as separate and independent state, with full power to levy war, conclude peace, contract alliances, establish commerce, and to do all other acts and things which independent States may of right do.

Source: *Rebellion Record*, Frank Moore, editor, New York: Arno Press, 1977, Volume 1, pp. 3-4.

Sojourner Truth

A freed slave, once called Isabella, named herself Sojourner Truth and traveled over the country giving speeches about slavery. She said, "I have borne five children and seen them all sold off into slavery, and when I cried out with a mother's grief, none but Jesus heard...." Following is a hymn that she composed.

I am pleading for my people,
A poor downtrodden race,
Who dwell in freedom's boasted land,
With no abiding place.

I am pleading that my people
May have their rights restored
For they have long been toiling,
And yet have no reward ...

Whilst I bear upon my body
The scars of many a gash,
I am pleading for my people
Who groan beneath the lash.

Source: Found in *Women in the Civil War: Warriors, Patriots, Nurses, and Spies*, edited by Phyllis Rabin Emert, Carlisle, MA: Discovery Enterprises, Ltd., 1995, p 12.

Summary:
My people are poor and they live in a land that brags about its freedoms. Yet my people have no place to call their own. I beg to have my people's rights given to them. They work very hard and get no rewards. I have scars on my body from many wounds [from beatings]. I plead for my people who also suffer under the whip.

Vocabulary:
abiding = permanent, lasting
gash = wound, cut
sojourner = visitor, traveler
whilst = while

Abraham Lincoln (Courtesy of Mediasource)

States Divided

President Lincoln did not want to go to war. He begged the Southern people to change their minds about living in slave states that were separated from the Union. But the South was determined to maintain its old way of life.

Lincoln's First Inaugural Address

Following are selected portions of Abraham Lincoln's inauguration speech, given in 1861.

Summary:
The Union [of the states] was formed in 1774. It has since been described and refined in the Declaration of Independence and the Constitution. Therefore, a single state cannot legally leave the Union. To secede is to break the law.

...the Union is perpetual... The Union is much older than the Constitution. It was formed in fact, by the Articles of Association in 1774. It was matured and continued by the Declaration of Independence in 1776. It was further matured ...by the Articles of Confederation in 1778. And finally, in 1787, ...the Constitution, was "to form a more perfect Union."

It follows from these views that no State, upon its own mere motion can lawfully get out of the Union, …and that acts of violence, within ally State or States, against the authority of the United States, are insurrectionary or revolutionary, according to circumstances.

· ·

…Physically speaking, we cannot separate. We cannot remove our respective sections from each other, nor build an impassable wall between them. A husband and wife may be divorced, and go…beyond the reach of each other; but the different parts of our country cannot do this. They cannot but remain face to face…. Can aliens make treaties easier than friends can make laws?

· ·

In your hands, my dissatisfied fellow-countrymen, and not in mine, is the momentous issue of civil war…. You can have no conflict, without being yourselves the aggressors. You have no oath registered in Heaven to destroy the government, while I shall have the most solemn one to "preserve, protect and defend" it.

Source: Lincoln's First Inaugural Address, March 4, 1861, from Stanley Appelbaum, ed., *Abraham Lincoln Great Speeches*, New York: Dover Publications, Inc., 1991, pp. 53-61.

Summary:
Our states cannot actually withdraw from one another. Their borders still touch. Husbands and wives can divorce and move away from each other. However, our states remain face to face, as enemies. Friends can make laws that satisfy each other. Enemies have great difficulty solving their problems.

A decision to start a civil war rests with you, the people: not me. War cannot exist unless someone attacks. My oath [promise] is to defend our government. There is no blessing from Heaven that supports your oath to destroy it.

Vocabulary:
aggressors = attackers
impassable = closed, impenetrable
momentous = very important
perpetual = never ending
respective = individual, specific

Southern Sentiments

Many people in the South felt that the cruelties of slavery described by the Northerners were not true. They were enraged that Northerners wanted to change their way of life.

Summary:

All of us in the South now think alike. Our shared anger with the Federal Government has brought us together. We want to resist the forces of the Government. Our Congress is acting like a tyrant. The Republican Party and Lincoln's Cabinet [advisors] make their own laws. They are making war against the Confederate [Southern] states without any law to back them up. Mr. Lincoln might as well do away with our Congress so that he and his friends can run our country however they wish.

Vocabulary:

abolished = done away
   with, destroyed
arrogating = seizing
   without justification
coercive = using force
fulminate = spit out,
   discharge
obliterated = wiped out
oligarchy = a government
   run by a small group of
   people

New Orleans Bulletin April 27, 1861

Public sentiment in the South has become a unit. …The coercive policy of the Black Republican Government has produced what nothing else could have done. It has obliterated all mere party differences in the Southern States, and brought all men upon the same platform of resistance to such coercion…. That power seems to have entirely forgotten that there is a legislative body known as Congress, for it is arrogating to itself as much authority as Louis Napoleon or the Emperor of Russia ever exercised. The Republican Cabinet has been converted into an oligarchy, wielding unlimited authority…. The Lincoln Cabinet, instead of merely carrying into effect the laws that Congress passes, makes laws of its own, or rather proceeds to make war upon the Confederate States without any law. Why don't Mr. Lincoln fulminate a decree declaring Congress abolished, and himself and his friends in perpetual authority, with power to do just what they like, law or no law? He might as well do this, as to do what he is doing.

Source: *Rebellion Record,* Frank Morse, editor, New York: Arno Press, 1977, p. 138.

The South as a Foreign Power

Many Northerners were afraid of what might happen if the Confederacy were a separate power from the Federal Government. Edward Everett was a powerful politician who made many speeches in support of the Union. He also supported the war, which he felt would end the Confederacy (if the North were victorious). Following are portions of his speech.

...if the Southern Confederacy is recognized, it becomes a Foreign Power, established along a curiously dove-tailed frontier of 1,500 miles, commanding some of the most important commercial and military positions and lines of communications for travel and trade; half the seacoast of the Union.... The seceding patriots of South Carolina were understood by the correspondent of the London "Times," to admit that they would rather be subject to a British prince, than to the Government of the United States. Whether they desire it or not, the moment the seceders lose the protection of the United States, they hold their independence at the mercy of the powerful governments of Europe. If the navy of the North should withdraw its protection, there is not a Southern State on the Atlantic or the Gulf, which might not be recolonized by Europe, in six months after the outbreak of a foreign war.

Source: Address by Edward Everett, "Secession Establishes a Foreign Power on the Continent." Found in *Rebellion Record*, Frank Morse, editor, New York: Arno Press, 1977, Vol 1, pp. 38-9.

Summary:

If the Government says that the Southern Confederacy is legal, it would then be called a Foreign Power. Half of the seacoast (about 1500 miles) of the Union would be under Confederate control. They would then have control of all the profitable trade and travel in this area.

They have said that they would rather be under British control than to be ruled by the Government of the United States. If they become a Foreign Power, they would lose the protection of the Federal government. Without that protection, the South could be ruled by a European Power within six months.

Vocabulary:
correspondent = writer
recolonized = taken over
   again

Civil War Begins

After South Carolina seceded, six more Southern states withdrew from the Union by February of 1861. These states quickly met and formed the Southern Confederacy. Jefferson Davis was their elected President. Later that year, four additional states joined the Confederacy. As each state seceded, it took over the Federal forts in its area. Both North and South began to activate their militias [reserve troops] and to call for volunteers.

Jefferson and Varina Davis (Library of Congress)

Jefferson Davis Seeks Recruits

In April 1861, after Lincoln had called for volunteers, Jefferson Davis asked for volunteers for his forces. Davis said that Lincoln intended to take back the Southern fortresses. He felt that the rights of the Confederacy had to be defended.

Vocabulary:

aggression = attack, invasion

issue = put out, send

proclamation = announcement

vessels = ships

wanton = reckless, wild

I, JEFFERSON DAVIS, President of the Confederate States of America, do issue this my Proclamation, inviting all those who may desire, by service in private armed vessels on the high seas, to aid this Government in resisting so wanton and wicked an aggression....

Source: *Rebellion Record,* Frank Morse, editor, New York: Arno Press, 1977, p.71.

Fort Sumter

Fort Sumter guarded the busy harbor at Charleston, North Carolina. The Civil War began when Confederate troops opened fire on the fort in April, 1861. Charleston citizens sat on the roofs of their homes and picnicked as they watched the "fireworks." General G. T. Beauregard sent the following message to Major Robert Anderson, who commanded the Federal soldiers occupying the fort.

Fort Sumter after its capture, showing damage from the Rebel bombardment of over 3000 shells and now flying the Rebel "Stars and Bars," April 14, 1861. (Library of Congress)

From Brigadier-General Beauregard's letter to Major Robert Anderson

Headquarters, Provisional Army, C.S.A.
Charleston, S.C., April 11, 1861 - 2 P.M.

...I am ordered by the Government of the Confederate States to demand the evacuation of Fort Sumter. My Aids, Colonel Chesnut and Captain Lee, are authorized to make such demand of you. All proper facilities will be afforded for the removal of yourself and command, together with company, arms, and property, and all private property, to any post in the United States which you may elect. The flag which you have upheld so long and with so much fortitude, under the most trying circumstances, may be saluted by you on taking it down....

Source: *Rebellion Record,* Frank Morse, editor, New York: Arno Press, 1977, pp. 50-1.

Summary:
My government demands that you leave. Rooms are available to assist you as you prepare to depart with all your soldiers, arms, and property. You may salute your flag that you have protected with great courage, before you take it down.

Vocabulary:
evacuation = removal
facilities = rooms, equipment
fortification = fortress
fortitude = courage, determination

We're Going to War

As the news of war spread over the country, people debated, discussed, and prepared for it. Both sides showed feelings of great confidence, hopefulness, and a fierce loyalty to their cause.

Consider This:

There were a number of instances where brothers or good friends chose to fight on opposite sides. In these instances, families were torn apart just as the country was torn apart.

Summary:

Public meetings are held about the war. People vote to keep the war going. Private citizens also give money. Everyone accepts that we are going to war. Some say it is to settle disagreements; others say it is a judgment from God.

Vocabulary:

alacrity = speed
cherished = held dear
controversy = argument
inevitable = unavoidable
mustered = gathered
sustain = keep going

An Indiana Farm Boy, April, 1861

Father and I were husking out some corn. When William Cory came across the field...he was excited and said, "Jonathan the Rebs have fired upon and taken Fort Sumpter." Father got white and couldn't say a word.

...Grandma wanted to know what was the trouble. Father told her and she began to cry. "Oh my poor children in the South! Now they will suffer!... Oh to think that I should have lived to see the day when Brother should rise against Brother."

Source: Henry Steele Commager, ed., *The Blue and the Gray.* New York: Wings Books, 1950, pp. 39-40.

Reactions in Boston, April 12, 1861

...Public meetings are held everywhere, in the small towns and villages as much as in the cities; considerable sums of money are voted to sustain the movement and take care of the families of those who are mustered into service; and still larger sums are given by individuals. Nobody holds back. Civil war is freely accepted everywhere; by some with alacrity, as the only means of settling a controversy based on long-cherished hatreds; by others as something sent as a judgment from Heaven, like a flood or an earthquake; by all as inevitable, by all as the least of the evils, among which we are permitted to choose....

Source: Ticknor and Hillard, eds., *Life, Letters, and Journals of George Ticknor.* Found in Henry Steele Commager, ed., *The Blue and the Gray*, New York: Wings Books, 1950, p. 41.

Georgians and the War

The day that Georgia was declared out of the Union…the general feeling was one of excitement and joy.

Then we began preparing our soldiers for the war. The ladies were all summoned to public places…and everybody who had sewing machines was invited to send them…. The sewing machines were sent to these places and ladies that were known to be experts in cutting out garments were engaged in that part of the work, and every lady in town was turned into a seamstress and worked as hard as anybody could work; and the ladies not only worked themselves but they brought colored seamstresses to these places, and these halls and public places would be filled with busy women all day long.

…of course there was a great deal of the pathetic manifested in connection with this enthusiasm, because we knew that the war meant the separation of our soldiers from their friends and families and the possibility of their not coming back. Still, while we spoke of these things, we really did not think that there was going to be actual war…. We got our soldiers ready for the field…. They were ordered to Virginia under the command of General Joseph E. Johnston. The young men carried dress suits with them and any quantity of fine linen….

Every soldier, nearly, had a servant with him, and a whole lot of spoons and forks, so as to live comfortably and elegantly….

Source: Congressional Testimony of Mrs. Mary A. Ward. Found in Milton Meltzer, *Voices From the Civil War*, New York: Harper Collins, 1989, pp. 34-6.

Consider This:
Remember: there was no television, no radio to keep the people up to date about the national events of war. Town meetings or speakers may or may not have produced accurate information. Some people had no idea they were preparing for a long, brutal war.

107th U. S. Colored Troops (Library of Congress)

Slaves in the War

General Henry Halleck, Commander-in-Chief of the Union army, sent the following letter to General Ulysses Grant. He described the army rules about the use of black soldiers. Halleck needed to caution his soldiers about showing prejudice [narrow-mindedness] towards former slaves. Not all Northerners were open-minded about equal treatment of freed slaves.

Summary:

It is quite all right to use black men to defend important holdings. When we need more soldiers in the New Orleans area, black men can be recruited to defend our bases on the Mississippi River.

Vocabulary:

depots = stations, bases
practicable = possible

General Henry Halleck

Washington (D.C.)

March 31st/63

...Again, it is the policy of the government to use the negroes of the South so far as practicable as a military force for the defense of forts, depots, etc. If the experience of Genl. Banks near New Orleans should be satisfactory, a much larger force will be organized during the coming summer; & if they can be used to hold points on the Mississippi during the sickly season, it will afford much relief to our armies.

They certainly can be used with advantage as laborers, teamsters, cooks, etc.

And it is the opinion of many who have examined the question without passion or prejudice, that they can also be used as a military force....

It has been reported to the Secretary of War that many of the officers of your command not only discourage the negroes from coming under our protection, but, by ill treatment, force them to return to their masters. This is not only bad policy in itself, but it is directly opposed to the policy adopted by the government....

It is expected that you will use your official and personal influence to remove prejudices on this subject, and to fully and thoroughly carry out the policy now adopted and ordered by the government. That policy is to withdraw from the use of the enemy all the slaves you can, and to employ those so withdrawn, to the best possible advantage against the enemy.

...The north must either destroy the slave-oligarchy, or become slaves themselves;...

Very respectfully Your obedient servant.

H.W. Halleck

Source: "General Henry Halleck's Letter to General Ulysses S. Grant Regarding Slaves," from Ira Berlin, editor, *Free at Last - A Documentary History of Slavery, Freedom, and the Civil War*, The New Press, 1992.

Summary:
They can be laborers, drivers, and cooks.

Black men should also be part of the regular army.

I hear that some of our soldiers are unkind to them. Our Government cannot approve of this behavior. Mistreated former slaves might return to their masters in the South. Or they might not serve our army well.

Our policy is to take as many slaves as possible away from the South, and use them wisely.

If we don't end slavery now, we might become slaves ourselves, as the workers [in our businesses] for the wealthy people of the South.

Vocabulary:
employ = use
oligarchy = a government
  in which the power is in
  the hands of a few
prejudice = narrow
  minded, intolerance
teamsters = drivers

General Robert E. Lee Resigns

General Robert E. Lee was asked to command the Union army as it was forming. Robert E. Lee was from Virginia. Since he did not want to take part in the invasion of his home state, he resigned from the Federal Army. In 1862, he became commander of the Army of Northern Virginia and was regarded as a great general by the Southerners. Following is a part of the letter he wrote to General Winfield Scott of the Union Army.

Summary:

Since I talked with you on the 18th, I have come to feel I can no longer stay in this army. Therefore, I resign [quit].

I shall remember your kindness until the day I die. If I did not feel I had to defend my state of Virginia, I would never fight again.

I wish you happiness and well being.

Robert E. Lee to General Winfield Scott

General:

Since my interview with you on the 18th instant I have felt that I ought not longer to retain my commission in the Army. I therefore render my resignation, which I request you will recommend for acceptance.

. . . .

I shall carry with me to the grave the most grateful recollections of your kind consideration, and your name and fame will always be dear to me. Save in defence of my native State, I never desire again to draw my sword.

Be pleased to accept my most earnest wishes for the continuance of your happiness and prosperity and believe me most truly yours.

R. E. Lee

Source: Clifford Dowdey, *Lee*. Boston: Little Brown & Company, 1965, p. 134.

Responding to Lincoln's Call

In July, 1862, Lincoln called for 300,000 more volunteers. James Gibbons, a Quaker and strong abolitionist, wrote a hymn in response to the call. Following are the first two verses.

We Are Coming, Father Abraham

We are coming, Father Abraham, three
  hundred thousand more,
From Mississippi's winding stream and from
  New England's shore;
We leave our ploughs and workshops, our
  wives and children dear,
With hearts too full for utterance, with but a
  silent tear;
We dare not look behind us, but steadfastly
  before:
We are coming, Father Abraham, three
  hundred thousand more!

If you look across the hill-tops that meet the
  northern sky,
Long moving lines of rising dust your vision
  may descry;
And now the wind, an instant, tears the
  cloudy veil aside,
And floats aloft our spangled flag in glory
  and in pride,
And bayonets in the sunlight gleam, and
  bands brave music pour,
We are coming, Father Abraham, three
  hundred thousand more!

Source: Henry Steele Commager, editor, *The Blue and the Gray*. New York: Wings Books, 1950, p. 574.

Summary:

We answer your call, President Lincoln. We come from across the country. We cannot look behind, where our loved ones wait. We look ahead, to the needs of our country.

We march over the hilltops; you can see the rising dust. Then, as the dust clears, you can see our [Union] flag. Our weapons glisten in the sun. We hear the passionate music of our country.

Vocabulary:

descry = notice, observe
spangled = decorated
steadfastly = faithfully,
  steadily
utterance = speaking;
  saying

Life at Home and On the Front

The South suffered from a shortage of supplies since most of America's industries were located in the North. The South, primarily rural [farm] country, had to depend on supplies sent from Europe. As the North captured Southern harbor-forts, they cut off in-coming European goods. It was called the Blockade.

Shortages and Rations

Rations [army food] became scarcer for both sides as the war dragged into its third and fourth year.

Consider This:

The people of the South learned how to save and use every natural resource to substitute for supplies no longer available. Do you think the people of today would know how to do the same thing?

Vocabulary:

contraband = illegal, smuggled goods
ovaries = pouches, sacs
servants = slaves
sorghum = a cereal plant with juice that can be made into syrup

Things Disappear

Almost at once we began to feel the pinch of war. White sugar disappeared immediately; not only were there no more lumps for gun-shy horses, but there was no sugar for the table. There was, however, an unlimited quantity of sorghum syrup, and around the barrels of sorghum, a thick crust of brown sugar often formed. This was carefully scraped off to be served with coffee and berries, the fluid product going to the servants.

In a very short time I noticed that matches had disappeared, and I have learned that at the outbreak of the war there was not one match factory in the South....

...Paper was getting so scarce that my elders feared that even the dreaded death lists might cease to come. Then it was discovered that wallpaper could be used....

The Government declared all drugs contraband of war, and almost no morphine or quinine came through the blockade. As a substitute for the latter, as I have already stated, we used boneset tea, which helped but did not cure malaria. To supply opiate we grew our own poppies, making incisions into the sides of the ovaries of these plants and with the flat of a case knife scraping up the exuded gum. The knife was then scraped off on the edge of a glass jar, and thus we found that we could raise gum opium that was 10 or 12 percent morphine.

There was a poppy bed in every garden planted for this purpose, and when I was seven years old I worked daily for the soldiers, scraping the…juice of the poppy…. I worked under the eternal mandate, "Don't taste it!" On some fifty poppy heads it was a morning's work to get a mass about as big as a small peanut.

The time came when no more Chilean nitre could run the blockade, and the South must depend on it own resources for this essential element of explosives. It was then that the urine cart began to make its rounds, collecting the night's urine and hauling it to the boiling vats, where the urea and other nitrogenous constituents were extracted and shipped to Augusta, Georgia, for the manufacture of gunpowder. That plant was never more than a few days ahead of the needs of the firing line.

Later on the need became so great that many old cabins which stood up on four corner posts were raised by levers, so that men could crawl under them to scrape the ground for the thin layer of nitrogen-charged clay at the top.… We heard that in Virginia and Kentucky searching parties invaded the caves where bats roosted, to scrape the bat manure from the floor. All such gleanings were likewise sent to the plant in Augusta.

Source: Thomas A. Bailey & David M. Kennedy, editors, *The American Spirit*, Volume I, 8th edition. Lexington, Massachusetts: D.C. Heath & Company, 1994, pp. 476-8.

Summary:

Everyone grew poppies. We cut into the plants' pouches and scraped the sticky stuff into a jar. We were then able to make morphine [pain medicine]. One morning's work with fifty poppy heads produced a chunk about as big as a peanut.

When we could no longer get nitre , we began to collect our urine. The urine was boiled to get ingredients for gunpowder, made in Augusta, Georgia. Men would scrape the ground under old cabins to get the nitrogen from the top layer. They even went to caves and scraped bat manure from the floor.

Vocabulary:
case knife = a large table knife
Chilean = from the country of Chile
constituents = ingredients, contents
exuded = oozing out
gleanings = gatherings
manufacture = making
nitre = potassium nitrate; used in gunpowder
punctured = opened; made a hole in

Summary:

Some people look like bums. Their clothes are torn and dirty. Some are thin and pale. Only the traders, and those in charge of supplies look well off.

My daughter fed a rat in the kitchen today. Soon other rats appeared; they seemed tame and thankful. We may have to eat the rats.

Vocabulary:

commissaries = those in charge of food and supplies

dilapidated = shabby

gaunt = thin

quartermasters = officers in charge of supplies

speculators = business traders

vagabonds = homeless people

A Journal of Shortages

December 1, 1862 — ...A portion of the people look like vagabonds. We see men and women and children in the streets in dingy and dilapidated clothes; and some seem gaunt and pale with hunger—the speculators, and thieving quartermasters and commissaries only, looking sleek and comfortable....

February 11, 1863—Some idea may be formed of the scarcity of food in this city from the fact that, while my youngest daughter was in the kitchen today, a young rat came out of its hole and seemed to beg for something to eat; she held out some bread, which it ate from her hand, and seemed grateful. Several others soon appeared, and were as tame as kittens. Perhaps we shall have to eat them!...

Source: Thomas A. Bailey & David M. Kennedy, editors, *The American Spirit*, Volume I, 8th edition. Lexington, Massachusetts: D.C. Heath & Company, 1994, pp. 475-6.

Sometimes soldiers did have to eat rats. This illustration drawn by a Confederate prisoner at Point Lookout Prison, shows the catching and cooking of rats. (National Archives)

The Washington Artillery of New Orleans, a famous Confederate group, which had organized in 1838 and fought in the Mexican War (National Archives)

Southern Rations

It is stated that after the first year of the war, the daily rations of a Confederate soldier when marching or fighting, were one pint of corn-meal, one-fourth pound of bacon. If camping, in addition to this he drew one-fourth pound of sugar, or one-half pint of molasses, three-fourths of a pound of black peas, one ounce of salt, and one-eighth of a pound of soap, and on Christmas Day, a jagger of pinetop whiskey.

...An ex-Confederate soldier told the writer that his daily ration for more than a week before the surrender at Appomattox, was an ear of corn for himself and three for his horse.

Source: James J. McDonald, *Life in Old Virginia*. Norfolk Virginia: The Old Virginia Publishing Company, 1907, p. 327.

Summary:
After the first year of war, Confederate soldiers were allowed one pint of cornmeal and one-fourth pound of bacon. In camp, they also got some sugar, molasses, salt, black peas, and soap. On Christmas they got a swallow of whiskey.

One soldier reported that during the last week of the war, he got one ear of corn for himself and three ears for his horse.

Vocabulary:
rations = food, meals

In his Diary of an Enlisted Man, *Lawrence Van Alstyne described cooking at the front: "The cook's house is simply a portion of the field we are in. A couple of crutches hold up a pole on which the camp kettles are hung and under which a fire is built."* (Library of Congress)

Consider This:

It appears that even though Union soldiers were hungry at times, they were better off than the Confederate soldiers.

A Union Army Kitchen

...When we are hungry we swallow anything that comes and are thankful for it.... The camp kettles are large sheet-iron pails, one larger than the other so one can be put inside the other when moving. If we have meat and potatoes, meat is put in one, and potatoes in the other.... The bread is cut into thick slices, and the breakfast call sounds. We grab our plates and cups, and wait for no second invitation. We each get a piece of meat and a potato, a chunk of bread and a cup of coffee with a spoonful of brown sugar in it. Milk and butter we buy, or go without.... We save a piece of bread for the last, with which we wipe up everything, and then eat the dish rag. Dinner and breakfast are alike, only sometimes the meat and potatoes are cut up and cooked together, which makes a really delicious stew. Supper is the same, minus the meat and potatoes.

Source: Lawrence Van Alstyne, *Diary of an Enlisted Man*. New Haven, Connecticut: Tuttle, Morehouse & Taylor Co., 1910, pp. 29-31.

Union and Confederate soldiers trade tobacco and coffee across a river. (J.O. Casler)

Making Coffee

Our coffee when we first went out was issued to us green, so that we had to roast and grind it, which was not always a success, some of it being burnt, while some would be almost green. In roasting it we put a quantity of it in a mess pan, and placing the pan over the fire would have to keep stirring it round with a stick in order to have it roasted as evenly as possible. These mess pans were used to fry our pork in and also as a wash basin. Our soup, coffee and meat were boiled in camp kettles suspended over the fire, which were also used for boiling our dirty clothes. Not a very nice thing for a soup pot, especially when they were full of vermin, as they were most of the time when on active service.

Source: Alfred Ballard, *Gone for a Soldier: The Civil War Memoirs of Private Alfred Ballard*. Boston: Little, Brown, and Co., 1975, p. 119.

Consider This:

Diseases killed more men on both sides than did wounds. Army officers knew little about good nutrition or how to keep a sanitary camp. A lot of soldiers suffered from dysentery [a severe disease of the bowels], which often resulted in death.

Goober Peas

"Goober Peas" was the popular name for peanuts, commonly grown in the South. Goober peas were a favorite food of the Confederate "mess mates" [soldiers who ate together]. This song is still sung today, recognized as a treasured folk song from Civil War times.

Sittin' by the roadside on a summer day,
Chattin' with my mess-mates passin' time away,
Lyin' in the shadow underneath the trees,
Goodness how delicious, eatin' goober peas.

Chorus:
Peas peas peas peas , eatin' goober peas.
Goodness how delicious, eatin' goober peas.

When a horseman passes, the soldiers have a rule,
To cry out at their loudest,"mister here's your
        mule,"
But another pleasure enchantinger than these,
Is wearin' out your grinders, eatin' goober peas.

Chorus

Just before the battle, the general hears a row,
He says "the yanks are comin', I hear their rifles
        now!"
He turns around in wonder and what d'ya think
        he sees,
The Georgia militia, eating goober peas.

Chorus

I think my song has lasted almost long enough,
The subject's interesting, but rhymes are mighty
        rough,
I wish this war was over when free from rags
        and fleas,
We'd kiss our wives and sweethearts and gobble
        goober peas.

Chorus

Source: Sung by Bobby Horton, *Songs of the C.S.A.,*
Homespun Records, Volume 3, 1987.

Into Battle

The North planned to capture forts along the Mississippi River to separate the western and eastern Confederate states. The Union also planned to create a naval blockade in the major Atlantic ports to deprive the Confederates of needed supplies from Europe. If necessary, the Union army also planned to march right through the middle of the Confederacy.

The South spent most of the time defending itself. Only a few major offensive battles were successful. The shortage of supplies, money and food contributed to the defeat of the South.

Guns

During the first year of the war the ordnance department succeeded in furnishing the various armies in the field…one million two hundred and seventy-six thousand six hundred and eighty-six portable firearms (muskets, carbines, and pistols), one thousand nine hundred and twenty-six field—or siege-guns, twelve hundred pieces for batteries in position, and two hundred and fourteen million cartridges for small-arms and for cannon. But it was obliged to apply to Europe for muskets and ammunition; this was the only war commodity that America procured in considerable quantities from the Old World, and it was this supply which proved to be the most defective.

Source: Notes on the war made by the Compte de Paris. Found in Henry Steele Commager, editor, *The Blue and the Gray*. New York: Wings Books, 1950, p. 99.

Summary:

Our government supplied us with all our weapons during the first year of war. They included small fire-arms, big guns for major attacks, bullets, and cannons. By the second year we had to order muskets and ammunition from Europe. The American-made firearms worked better than the imported ones.

Vocabulary:

ammunition = bullets
batteries = groups of field soldiers
carbines = guns used by the land troops
cartridges = bullets
commodity = goods, merchandise
defective = not working right, damaged
muskets = a large firearm, shorter than the rifle
ordnance = weapons

31

Fighting Hand-to-Hand

A captain, I think of a New York regiment, ran up to me and grabbing the flagstaff called out to me, "You damned little rebel, surrender." I held on and jerked him to me, striking at him at the same time with my sword, which was hung to my wrist by a sword knot. He at once jumped back and fired at me with his pistol, cursing me all the time and tugging at the flagstaff. I kept jerking it back and striking at him with my sword, while at the same time struggling to get from under my dead horse, which was lying on my legs.

One ball from the pistol struck the star of my collar and burned my neck like fire, while another struck my little finger, breaking it and smashing a seal ring which I wore. Another just grazed my leg, but that one felt like a double-heated, hot iron, and made me struggle so that I found myself free from my horse and on my feet.

Our troops by this time were pouring in and the Yankees running, my opponent among them. But he was a little too late, and I caught up with him. I cut down on him with both hands, expecting to split him, as we used to read of in novels, but my sword bounced off him, knocking him to his knees. He rose and turned, facing with his pistol in his hands. I never doubted but that he was about to shoot again and ran him through. He lived only a few minutes, trying to say something. I told him that I would send his effects to his people, which was apparently what he was trying to ask.

Source: John Haskell, *The Haskell Memoirs*. New York: G. P. Putnam's Sons, 1960, pp. 33-4.

Ways of Death

More than 600,000 men and boys died during the Civil War. Those who were lucky enough to return home told incredible stories about what they had seen. Some of the most touching tales described the death of one person, instead of huge numbers lying on the battlefield.

Death on the Battlefield

Of two brothers, Corporals Samuel and Joseph B. Ruhl, one was killed in the battle, and the other had to march away leaving him upon the field. Word was sent to the family that Joseph was killed. His sister Sarah, on receiving the sad news, said that she would go and bring him home. Ordering two horses hitched to a spring wagon, she started on her mournful journey, and by night of the same day on which she received the news of his death she was many miles on her way towards Gettysburg. Reaching the battlefield, she began the search for his body, or, rather, his grave, as he had been buried in the meantime. After a long search she found it, had the body unearthed, and placing it in a coffin conveyed it home, where it was laid to rest in the quiet graveyard by the side of the fields through which he roamed in boyhood days.

Source: Thomas Chamberlain, *History of the One Hundred and Fiftieth Regiment Pennsylvania Volunteers.* Philadelphia: J.B. Lippincott Co., 1895, p. 155.

(Library of Congress)

Consider This:

It is hard to imagine that a family member could travel from home and reach a battlefield in a day's time. In some war-torn countries in this world, this still happens. But since the Civil War, the United States has fought in wars that have been far away.

Vocabulary:
conveyed = transported, carried
mournful = sad, unhappy
unearthed = dug up

Consider This:
Bodies lay everywhere on the battlefields throughout the South.

Family members often had to search for the bodies of loved ones themselves if they wanted to bring them home to be buried.

Activity:
Talk about why this
was such a dreadful
form of death, compared
to seeing many bodies
on a battlefield.

Vocabulary:
condemned = sentenced,
 doomed
deserter = a military
 runaway
execution = putting to
 death
massed = gathered
reprieve = pardon,
 postponement
secured = tied
unconsciously = unaware

Military Execution

No medical experience or interest could prevent the fatal result of thousands of wounds and diseases, which under more favoring circumstances could have been cured. I have seen death in many forms—once and once only in its most dreadful form, a military execution. A deserter had been brought back from the North, tried and condemned to be executed. Twenty thousand men were massed upon three sides of a hollow square. Around this square he passed, his arms secured behind him, soldiers with bayoneted muskets before and behind him, the band playing the Dead March, while the guards kept time to the music, in the sight of all the soldiers. Apparently he had been thoroughly drilled, for he was keeping step with the guard, I turned to the officer sitting on his horse beside me, and exclaimed, "See that man unconsciously keeping time to his own death march." He looked from side to side, apparently hoping up to the last moment for the reprieve which was never to come; the guard stopped beside his coffin, his back was turned towards the firing squad, the lieutenant in charge dropped the handkerchief, the fatal shots riddled his body, and he fell dead across his own coffin.

Source: Major Albert Gailard Hart, M.D., *The Surgeon and the Hospital in the Civil War*. Gaithersburg, Maryland: Olde Soldier Books, Inc., 1987.

Night on the Battlefield

The dark shadows of night at last fell upon the awful scene of carnage and the turmoil of battle gradually died away, leaving only the watchful, warning shots along the confronting lines of pickets. Both sides were well nigh exhausted, but still defiantly confronting each other upon nearly the same ground as when the battle had commenced two days before. The tired men dropped upon the ground for rest and sleep, the living and dead lying side by side.... [I wondered] if the light of coming day would witness a renewal of the struggle.

. . . .

The glories of war were lost in its sickening sights. The gay parade, with the old-time flag gracefully floating in the evening breeze, the nodding plumes, gaudy uniforms with brightly polished buttons, which were the admiration of the fair sex, the inspiring notes of the military band and all the pomp and glamour of war that shone so beautifully as the regiment marched out from their home camp for embarkation, had lost their charms for him....

Source: Warren Wilkinson, *Mother, May You Never See the Sights I Have Seen: The Fifty-Seventh Massachusetts Veteran Volunteers in the Last Year of the Civil War.* New York: Quill, 1990, p. 87.

Summary:

At last, night came and concealed the terrible sights of death. The battle noises stopped and we could only hear the warning shots of the watchmen. We had been fighting over the same ground for two days. Tired men dropped to the ground and slept among the dead. I wondered if it would start all over in the morning.

The memories of the parade, our uniforms with bright buttons, the exciting music, and the admiration of our women were gone. The glories of war had been conquered by the horrors of war.

Vocabulary:

carnage = bloodshed, mass murder
commenced = started
embarkation = departure
gaudy = flashy, showy
gay parade = jolly, happy
nigh = nearly
pickets = watchmen, lookout people
turmoil = disorder, confusion
witness = see

Sherman's March

In 1864, General W. T. Sherman, with 60,000 Union soldiers, conquered Atlanta, Georgia. In November, Sherman's men burned the city to the ground before they continued their march through Georgia to the sea. He and his soldiers, known as "Bummers" because they lived off the land, destroyed everything in their path. They wanted to crush the spirit of the South as well as destroy any property that might be useful to the Confederate troops.

Studio portrait of William Tecumseh Sherman

Consider This:

The civilians felt frightened and helpless as the tough, mean-spirited soldiers marched through their communities and destroyed everything.

Vocabulary:

cussedness = wickedness

feller = man

illustrate = explain by example

Bummers Described by a Correspondent

…They appear to be possessed of spirit of "pure cussedness." One incident of many will illustrate: A bummer stepped into house and inquired for sorghum. The lady of the house presented a jug, which he said was too heavy; so he merely filled his canteen. Then taking a huge wad of tobacco from his mouth, he thrust it into the jug. The lady inquired, in wonder, why he spoiled that which he did not want. "Oh, some feller'll come along and taste that sorghum, and think that you've poisoned him; then he'll burn your damned old house."

Source: Edward A. Pollard, *The Lost Cause.* New York: E. B. Treat & Co. Publishers, 1867, p. 664.

After Sherman's March
Described by Eliza Andrews

December 24, 1864— ...There was hardly a fence left standing.... The fields were trampled down and the road was lined with carcasses of horses, hogs, and cattle that the invaders, unable either to consume or to carry away with them, had wantonly shot down, to starve out the people and prevent them from making their crops. The stench in some places was unbearable....

The dwellings that were standing all showed signs of pillage, and on every plantation we saw the charred remains of [buildings] ...here and there lone chimney-stacks....

Hay ricks and fodder stacks were demolished, corn-cribs were empty, and every bale of cotton that could be found was burned by the savages. I saw no grain of any sort, except little patches they had spilled when feeding their horses....

Crowds of Confederate soldiers were tramping over the road in both directions.... They were mostly on foot, and I saw numbers seated on the roadside greedily eating raw turnips, meat skins, parched corn—anything they could find, even picking up the loose grains that Sherman's horses had left....

Source: Eliza F. Andrews, *The War-Time Journal of a Georgia Girl*. New York: D. Appleton and Company, 1908, pp. 32-3.

Summary:
The fences were down and the fields were flattened. Animal bodies were scattered everywhere, shot and then left by soldiers who could not eat them or carry them away. The stink was terrible. Every home, every building, was partly or completely destroyed.

The hay and feed storage bins were smashed and the corncribs were empty. The cotton bales were burned.

Confederate soldiers were walking the area in all directions. They were eating anything they could find: raw turnips, meat skins, dried corn, even loose grains left by Sherman's horses.

Vocabulary:
carcasses = dead bodies
charred = burned
consume = eat, devour
demolished = smashed, wrecked
pillage = destruction
stench = stink, bad odor
wantonly = shamelessly

Women and the War

The women of the Civil War were as willing and able to fight for what they believed in, as were the men. They were spies, writers, public speakers, and freedom fighters. They were also conductors on the Underground Railroad, nurses, and volunteers on the front lines, assisting with the sick and wounded soldiers.

Long before the war began, women were active as Abolitionists, trying to convince others of the evils of slavery. In the excerpts below, Angelina Grimké, a Southern woman with strong religious beliefs, spoke out about slavery, trying to capture the attention and support of Christian women of the South. Her comments came 25 years before the war began.

Summary:
It's sinful to hold people in bondage (as slaves) whether they were enslaved in Africa or in the Carolinas. (Referring to the Declaration of Independence) These are the rights that are given to all men, even though some people say they have title-deeds to their slaves and think they own them.

Vocabulary:
insurrections = uprisings, revolts
vengence (vengeance) = retaliation

Appeal to the Christian Women of the South
...in principle it is as sinful to hold a human being in bondage who has been born in Carolina, as one who has been born in Africa.... We must come back to the good old doctrine of our forefathers who declared to the world, "all men are created equal, and that they have certain inalienable rights among which are life, liberty, and the pursuit of happiness."

...If then, we have no right to enslave an African, surely we can have none to enslave an American; if it is a self evident truth that all men, every where and of every color are born equal, and have an inalienable right to liberty, then it is equally true that no man can be born a slave, and no man can ever rightfully be reduced to involuntary bondage and held as a slave, however fair may be the claim of his master or mistress through wills and title-deeds.

. . . .

Slavery always has, and always will produce insurrections, wherever it exists, because it is a violation of the natural order of things, and no human power can much longer perpetuate it. The opposers of abolitionists fully believe this; one of them remarked to me not long since, there is no doubt there will be a most terrible overturning at the South in a few years, such cruelty and wrong, must be visited with divine vengeance soon....

But I will now say a few words on the subject of Abolitionism.

Doubtless you have all heard Anti-Slavery societies denounced.... It has been said they publish the most abominable untruths, and that they are endeavoring to excite rebellions at the South. Have you believed these reports, my friends? ...Listen to me, then.... You know that I am a Southerner; you know that my dearest relatives are now in a slave State.... As a Carolinian, ...before I would join an Anti-Slavery Society, I took the precaution of becoming acquainted with some of the leading Abolitionists, of reading their publications and attending their meetings, at which I heard addresses both from colored and white men; and it was not until I was fully convinced that their principles were entirely pacific, and their efforts only moral, that I gave my name as a member to the Female Anti-Slavery Society of Philadelphia. Since that time, I have regularly taken the *Liberator*, and read many Anti-Slavery pamphlets and papers and books, and can assure you I...never read any account of cruelty which I could not believe. Southerners may deny the truth of these accounts, but why do they not prove them to be false.... I lived too long in the midst of slavery, not to know what slavery is....

. . . .

I have endeavored to set before you the exceeding sinfulness of slavery, and to point you to the example of those noble women who have been raised up in the church to effect great revolutions, and to suffer for the truth's sake. I have appealed to your sympathies as women, to your sense of duty as Christian women. I have attempted to vindicate the Abolitionists, to prove the entire safety of immediate Emancipation, and to plead the cause of the poor and oppressed.

Source: Angelina Grimké *Appeal to the Christian Women of the South* (1836); http.//www.furman.edu/~benson/docs/#

Summary:
People will always revolt against slavery. One person who opposes the Abolitionist movement told me she recognizes that someday the South will see slavery overturned. Before joining the Female Anti-Slavery Society, I looked into what abolitionists say and do, and they're telling the truth about the evils of slavery. I read their literature. I appeal to you as Christian women to support the causes of the abolition of slavery.

Vocabulary:
abominable = hateful
endeavored = tried
oppressed = crushed
vindicate = exonerate, clear

Women as Spies

Women who served as spies risked their lives at each meeting with the enemy or trip behind enemy lines. Rose O'Neal Greenhow, known as Rebel Rose, lived in Washington. As the widow of Dr. Robert Greenhow, she knew many important politicians and military men, and used her connections to gather information about the Union army for Confederate General Beauregard. He won an important victory at Bull Run, partly because of the spy ring that Rebel Rose led. She was eventually placed under house arrest for five months.

Rose O'Neal Greenhow and her daughter.

Consider This:

After her house arrest, Rose O'Neal Greenhow was transferred to a prison where she stayed for another six months. After her release, she was sent to England and France to gather allies and support for the Confederacy. When she was returning from Europe, she drowned when her boat overturned.

Vocabulary:

chamber = bedroom
resolved = vowed, decided
wardrobes = cabinets for clothing

Rose O' Neal Greenhow

On Friday, Aug. 23, 1861, as I was entering my own door ... I was arrested by two men, one in citizens clothes and the other in the dress of an officer of the United States Army.... Men also surrounded [the house] like bees from a hive. Men rushed with frantic haste into my chamber. My beds, my wardrobes were all up-turned. My library was taken possession of and every scrap of paper was seized ...

...I was allowed to go to my chamber and I then resolved to destroy some important papers which I had in my pocket.... On Friday the 30th of August I was informed that my house was to be converted into a prison ...

Source: Rose O'Neal Greenhow, *My Imprisonment and the First Year of Abolition Rule at Washington*. Found in *Heroines of Dixie*, by Jones. Bobbs-Merril Company, 1955, pp 62-6. (Originally published in 1864)

Battlefield Helpers and Nurses

On battlefields, women attended to the sick, wounded and dying. They saw terrible sights, but looked past the horror to give aid and comfort to those who needed it. Sarah Emma Edmonds ran away from home when she was 17, to escape an arranged marriage. She cut her hair and dressed like a man in order to enjoy freedom and privileges that women did not have in those days. In 1861, she enlisted with the Michigan volunteers as a male field nurse.

Sarah Emma Edmonds

The first man I saw killed was a gunner.... A shell had burst in the midst of the battery, killing one and wounding three men and two horses.... I stooped over one of the wounded, who, lay upon his face weltering in his blood.... The stretchers were soon brought, and he was carried from the field ...

Now the battle began to rage with terrible fury. Nothing could be heard save the thunder of artillery, the clash of steel, and the continuous roar of musketry....

...The sight of that field is perfectly appalling; men tossing their arms wildly calling for help; there they lie bleeding, torn and mangled. ...Two Rebel regiments of fresh troops are sent to make a flank movement.... They march through the woods, reach the top of the hill, and ... fire almost upon the backs of the gunners... Men and horses went down in an instant....

The news of this disaster spread along our lines like wildfire; officers and men were alike confounded; regiment after regiment broke and ran, and almost immediately the panic commenced ...

Source: Sarah Emma Edmonds, *Unsexed, or The Female Soldier,* also titled *Nurse and Spy in the Union Army.* Found in *Noble Women of the North,* edited by Dannett, New York: Thomas Yoseloff Publishers, 1959, pp. 110, 113-7.

Consider This:

It would require great strength of mind to concentrate on a task (for example, wrapping a wound) on a battlefield. The noises of shells bursting and gunfire would overwhelm most people. The added sights of men running in all directions, terrible wounds, and panic breaking out everywhere would be so distracting that some people could not do anything but stare in a state of terror.

Vocabulary:

appalling = shocking, frightful
confounded = dazed, confused
flank movement = around-the-side movement
mangled = twisted, crippled
weltering = rolling, wallowing

Ambulance rescue workers of the Army of the Potomac practice removing injured soldiers from the battlefield in a training program, 1862. (National Archives)

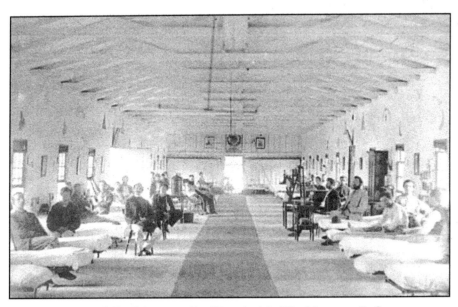

Patients in Ward K of Armory Sq. Hospital in Washington, D.C.

Louisa May Alcott

Louisa May Alcott, a well-known author, volunteered to work in a Washington Hospital in 1863. The following comes from her letters to her family.

The first thing I met was a regiment of the vilest odors that ever assaulted the human nose … everyone had assured me that it was a chronic weakness of all hospitals, and I must bear it. I did, armed with lavender water…

…In they came, some on stretchers, some in men's arms, some feebly staggering along propped on rude crutches, and one lay stark and still with covered face, as a comrade gave his name to be recorded before they carried him away to the dead house. All was hurry and confusion; the hall was full of these wrecks of humanity…the walls were lined with rows of such as could sit, the floor covered with the more disabled, the steps and doorways filled with helpers and lookers on; the sound of many feet and voices made that usually quiet hour as noisy as noon; and, in the midst of it all, the matron's motherly face brought more comfort to many a poor soul, than the cordial draughts she administered, or the cheery words that welcomed all, making of the hospital a home.

The sight of several stretchers, each with its legless, armless, or desperately wounded occupant, entering my ward, admonished me that I was there to work, not to wonder or weep; so I corked up my feelings.…

Source: Louisa May Alcott, *Hospital Sketches*. Edited by Jones. Massachusetts: The Belknap Press of Harvard University, 1960, pp. 29-30. (Originally published in 1864)

Consider This:
The hospital where she worked had been a hotel. The ward [a room full of beds] where she spent much of her time used to be the ballroom. After working in the hospital for six weeks, she was forced to leave because she developed a severe fever.

Vocabulary:
admonished = warned
chronic = constant, never ending
cordial draughts = warm-hearted doses of medicine
regiment = set, collection
stark = stiff
wrecks of humanity = injured, damaged men

On the Homefront

Every woman in the country was affected by the war, and most women helped out in whatever way they could, and did whatever they had to do to survive. Myrta Avary, married to a Confederate colonel, lived in Virginia.

Consider This:

Avary reported that even though there were times when they had almost nothing to eat, they were grateful to be alive. She said she never believed the people of the South would be defeated.

Vocabulary:

rations = food

scant = scarce

substantial = solid, filling

Source: Myrta L. Avary (also known as Nellie Grey), in *Ladies of Richmond*, by Jones. New York: Bobbs-Merrill Company, 1962, pp. 258-62.

Myrta L. Avary

We had become so poor and had so little to cook that we did most of our cooking ourselves over the grate, each woman often cooking her own rations ... Sometimes we would all get so hungry that we would put together all the money we could rake and scrape and buy a bit of roast or something else substantial and have a feast....

Sometimes our guests were boys from camp who dropped in and took stewed apples or boiled peas, as the case might be. If we were particularly fortunate we offered a cup of tea sweetened with sugar. The soldier who dropped in always got a part—and the best part—of what we had. If things were scant we had smiles to make up for the lack of our larder, and to hide its bareness.

Of course, children were affected by the war, too, and some, like Tillie Pierce, wrote about their experiences years later.

Vocabulary:

brandishing = waving menacingly

consternation = dismay and confusion

Source: Mrs. Tillie (Pierce) Alleman, *At Gettysburg or What a Girl Saw and Heard of the Battle. A True Narrative.* New York: 1889. Chpt.II, pp. 21-30.

"The Rebels are coming! The Rebels are coming!" was passed from lip to lip, and all was again consternation. We were having our regular literary exercises on Friday afternoon, ...when the cry reached our ears....Our teacher, ... at once said: "Children, run home as quickly as you can."...It did not require repeating....

What a horrible sight! There they were, human beings! clad almost in rags, covered with dust, riding wildly... down the hill toward our home! shouting, yelling most unearthly, cursing, brandishing their revolvers, and firing right and left.

War Comes to an End

In early 1865, the North was closing in on a victory. In January, the Congress passed the 13th Amendment to the Constitution, abolishing [ending] slavery. The Confederate capitol, Richmond, Virginia, finally fell to the North and Lee's army retreated. General Lee surrendered on April 9, at Appomattox, Virginia. The last Southern army surrendered to General Sherman in late April. However, celebration in the North was cut short when President Lincoln was shot on April 14. He died the following day.

Economic Disaster in the South

The North had more money, soldiers, supplies, and a better transport system than the South, even at the start of the war. But the South really suffered most when the North conquered its ports, cutting off supplies from Europe.

Notes from a *Rebel War Clerk's Diary*

January 18, 1863.— We are now, in effect, in a state of siege, and none but the opulent, often those who have defrauded the government, can obtain a sufficiency of food and raiment.…

These evils might be remedied by the government, for there is no great scarcity of any of the substantials and necessities of life in the country, if they were only equally distributed. The difficulty is in procuring transportation, and the government monopolizes the railroads and canals.

Source: John Beauchamp Jones, *Rebel War Clerk's Diary*. From Henry Steele Commager, editor, *The Blue and the Gray*. New York: Wings Books, 1950, pp. 744-7.

Summary:

We are now under constant attack. None but the wealthy, or those who cheat the government can get enough food or clothes. The government could fix these problems; there is enough food for everyone. However, supplies are not sent to us in the South. The government uses the railroads and the canals [boats] to carry supplies for the North only.

Vocabulary:

defrauded = cheated
monopolizes = uses all
opulent = rich, wealthy
procuring = getting
remedied = fixed
raiment = clothes
siege = constant attacks

Federal Troops Conquer and Loot

The people of the South were so weakened by their losses that they were unable to stand up to the victorious soldiers who marched into their towns.

Summary:

Soldiers would visit houses every day. Some begged for food and others demanded it. Some would push their way in, and even hit the owner with their pistols.

They would insist we give them money or anything valuable. If they saw a nice piece of jewelry, they would yank it away from the owner. They would hit us if we resisted.

Pickpockets roamed the streets. They would often approach someone and ask for the time. When the owner pulled out his watch, the pickpocket would snatch it or, if necessary, pull out a gun.

Vocabulary:

appropriation = taking
civilly = politely
conspicuously = openly, obviously
incontinently = with no control of cruel feelings
intimation = clue, hint
meek = humble, gentle
plucked = picked, yanked

At an early hour in the day, almost every house was visited by groups, averaging in number from two to six persons. Some of these entered civilly enough,... in some cases, begging for milk, eggs, bread and meat—in most cases, demanding them. In the house, parties less meek of temper than these pushed their way, and the first intimation of their presence ... was a pistol clapped at the head or bosom of the owner, whether male or female.

"Your watch!" "Your money!" was the demand. Frequently, no demand was made. Rarely, indeed, was a word spoken, where the watch or chain, or ring or bracelet, presented itself conspicuously to the eye. It was incontinently plucked away from the neck, breast or bosom.... The slightest show of resistance provoked violence to the person....

In the open streets the pickpockets were mostly active. A frequent mode of operating was by asking you the hour. If thoughtless enough to reply, producing the watch or indicating its possession, it was quietly taken from hand or pocket, and transferred to the pocket of the "other gentleman," with one such remark as this: "A pretty little watch that. I'll take it myself; it just suits me." And the appropriation followed; and if you hinted any dislike to the proceeding, grasp was taken of your collar, and the muzzle of a revolver put to your ear....

Source: Edward A. Pollard, *The Lost Cause.* New York: E.B. Treat & Co., pp. 666-7.

Richmond Burns

Richmond fell in early April, 1865. Since it was the capitol of the Confederacy, its fall signaled the near-end of the war. North and South had been battling over the possession of this city for some time. Before they escaped, Richmond citizens burned what they did not want the Union soldiers to have.

...The two cities, Richmond and Manchester, were like a blaze of day amid the surrounding darkness....

By daylight on the 3rd, a mob of men, women, and children, to the number of several thousands, had gathered at the corner of 14th and Cary streets ... attracted by the vast commissary depot at that point.... The depot doors were forced open and a demoniacal struggle for the countless barrels of hams, bacon, whiskey, flour, sugar, coffee, etc., etc., raged about the buildings among the hungry mob. The gutters ran whiskey, and it was lapped as it flowed down the streets, while all fought for a share of the plunder. The flames came nearer and nearer, and at last caught in the commissariat itself.

At daylight the approach of the Union forces could be plainly discerned. After a little came the clatter of horses' hoofs galloping up Main Street....

The engineer officer, Dr. Lyons, and I walked leisurely to the island, setting fire to the provided combustible matter as we passed along, and leaving the north section of Mayo's bridge wrapped in flame and smoke. We...saw a line of blue-coated horsemen galloping in furious haste up Main Street...and...dash down 14th Street to the flaming bridge. They fired a few random shots at us three on the island, and we retreated to Manchester.

Source: Philip Van Doren Stern, *An End to Valor*. Boston: Houghton Mifflin Company, 1958, pp. 179-81.

Summary:

Richmond and Manchester were lit up [by fire]. By morning, a large crowd forced open the doors of a big supply station. They fought each other for the whiskey, sugar, etc. Finally, the station caught fire.

At daylight, Union soldiers could be seen approaching. Three of us walked to the island, setting fire to anything that would burn, as we went. One part of the bridge was wrapped in flames and smoke. We saw soldiers on horses galloping as fast as they could toward the bridge. They fired a few shots at us and we fled to Manchester.

Vocabulary:

combustible = burnable
commissary depot = food
  and supply station
demoniacal = devilish
lapped = licked
plunder = stolen goods
random = hit-or-miss

Surrender

In February, representatives from the South had an informal meeting with President Lincoln to discuss an ending to the war. Lincoln wanted peace, but he was not willing to allow slavery or independent governments to exist.

Consider This:

The Confederate President, Jefferson Davis, left Richmond on April 2, as Union troops captured the city. He wrote this proclamation three days later. A month after that, he was captured in Georgia.

Vocabulary:

infamous = bad, shameful
Providence = destiny, fate

Jefferson Davis' Proclamation

Danville, Virginia, April 5, 1865

...I will never consent to abandon to the enemy one foot of the soil of any of the States of the Confederacy. That...Virginia, with the help of the people, and by the blessing of Providence, *shall be held and defended*, and no peace ever be made with the infamous invaders of her territory.... — Jefferson Davis

Source: Edward A. Pollard, *The Lost Cause*. New York: E.B. Treat & Co. Publishers, 1867, pp. 664, 701.

General Robert E. Lee also fled Richmond as it was falling. He surrendered at the Appomattox Courthouse in Virginia, ten days later.

Summary:

After four years of hard service, the Army of Northern Virginia must surrender to the North.

...further fighting would not be worth the continued loss of men so loved by their people.

Vocabulary:

arduous = hard, difficult
endeared = made beloved
fortitude = courage
unsurpassed = unequaled
valor = bravery
yield = give in

Lee's Farewell

Headquarters Army Northern Virginia,
April 10, 1865

After four years of arduous service, marked by unsurpassed courage and fortitude, the Army of Northern Virginia has been compelled to yield to overwhelming numbers and resources.

... feeling that valour and devotion could accomplish nothing that could compensate for the loss that would have attended the continuation of the contest, I have determined to avoid the useless sacrifice of those whose past services have endeared them to their countrymen.

Source: Edward A. Pollard, *The Lost Cause*. New York: E.B. Treat & Co. Publishers, 1867, p. 711.

Lincoln's Second Inaugural Address

Lincoln lived long enough to see the South failing, and to know that the war would soon come to an end. Following is a portion of his famous speech given at the time he was inaugurated as President for the second term.

With malice toward none; with charity for all; with firmness in the right, as God gives us to see the right, let us strive on to finish the work we are in; to bind up the nation's wounds; to care for him who shall have borne the battle, and for his widow, and his orphan — to do all which may achieve and cherish a just and lasting peace, among ourselves, and with all nations.

Source: Abraham Lincoln, "Second Inaugural Address." From Henry Steele Commager, editor, *The Blue and the Gray*, New York: Wings Books, 1950, pp. 1100-1.

Consider This:

Lincoln never wavered [doubted himself] in his belief that all the states had to be united under one government and that slavery had to end. Many believe that his strong convictions contributed to the Northern victory.

Vocabulary:

interior = inside
malice = bad feelings, ill will
recover = get better
restore = bring back
strive = try, attempt

The Battle Hymn

Julia Ward Howe, a famous poet and abolitionist, wrote the words to this hymn in 1861. She was inspired to write the poem after hearing the tune to another song called, "John Brown's Body." She felt the tune needed to have more powerful words. Later, the poem was printed in a widely circulated magazine, and the Union troops started singing it as they marched to war.

The hymn is still sung today, and believed to be a great patriotic song for the entire country.

The Battle Hymn of the Republic
by Julia Ward Howe

Mine eyes have seen the glory of the coming
of the Lord
He is trampling out the vintage where the
grapes of wrath are stored;
He hath loosed the fateful lightning of his
terrible swift sword,
His truth is marching on.

(Chorus: repeat after each verse.)
Glory! Glory! Hallelujah! Glory, Glory!
Hallelujah!
Glory! Glory! Hallelujah! His truth is march-
ing on.

In the beauty of the lilies Christ was born
across the sea,
With a glory in His bosom that transfigures
you and me;
As He died to make men holy, let us die to make
men free,
While God is marching on.

Chorus

Source: Henry Steele Commager, ed., *The Blue and The Gray*. New York: Wings Books, 1950, pp. 572-3.

Afterword

The Civil War was followed by a twelve-year period called Reconstruction. The North and South held fierce debates about how former slaves should be treated: their need for education, work and housing, civil rights, and more had to be decided. African Americans did not enjoy equal rights at the end of the war. They lived and went to school and to church in separate places in the South. Good work opportunities were not available for former slaves in the South, and the transition to freedom from slavery was a difficult one. White Southerners still wanted to rule their own states without interference from the Federal Government, and racist organizations like the Ku Klux Klan harassed and threatened the Black population for decades.

However, the war did bring an end to secession from the Union and legally brought an end to slavery. Even though Blacks (and other minority groups) still fight for equal rights today, they are protected against slavery by the 13th Amendment to the Constitution, adopted in December of 1865. Not long after, the adoption of the 14th Amendment (July 1868) protected basic rights such as voting, and owning property for former slaves—and for all citizens.

The devastation, death, and destruction of the Civil War is a fascinating chapter in our nation's military, economic, and social history. This war, more than any other in which Americans have been involved, affected the entire nation. More scholars and history buffs continue to study its battles and its leaders than any other war in our history. It has left us a legacy of rich folklore and patriotic music, a new appreciation of photojournalism and map-making skills, and a fascination and a passion for military maneuvers and local history that are unequaled. This small volume of memoirs of some of the participants and observers of the war will hopefully whet the appetite of the reader to delve further into the voluminous records of the battles, strategies, and daily lifestyles of those who fought in the War between the States.

Research Activities/Things to Do

- Harriet Beecher Stowe's *Uncle Tom's Cabin* was published in 1852. This widely-read book was an outcry for abolition and human rights that moved many people, both black and white, to take a stand against slavery. Find documentation in old newspapers on the reaction to the book in the mid-1800s.

- What was the main objective of the Union in the war?

- What was the main objective of the Confederacy in the war?

- How was the Civil War unlike any other war fought by Americans?

- If Lincoln had recognized states' rights, the Civil War might never have happened. Explain.

- Lincoln passed on the responsibility for war to the Southern states. He said they must return to the Union or face a war. What might have happened if the Confederacy had agreed to return to the Union at that time?

- Lincoln believed that a divided country would be the end of "free government upon the face of the earth." How would a divided nation have been viewed by foreign countries?

- Why did Southerners believe that slavery was protected under the Constitution?

- The Confederate states believed that foreign powers would recognize them as states independent of the United States. Why would they have assumed this?

- Evaluate this Confederate document:

  "I think now is the darkest of the war. I hope it will not last long from present indications. France will recognize us as independent and the North will be at war with England and France that is if there is any confidence to be placed in the papers if war does break out between the United States and foreign powers. The North can't whip us all and I think she will acknowledge our independence too.

  — Jasper W. Wilson to L. Ann Wilson,
  Sunday, September 27, 1863.
  Camp 4 miles from Mobile, Alabama"

- The Confederacy was forced to issue its own currency, create a new government structure, and more. Research the process by which all of these forced changes came about.

- More American soldiers died in the Civil War than in any other war in history. The Confederacy also had more deserters than ever before or since. Why do you think this happened? (Consider the words of the Confederate soldier below.)

> "Aug. 13, 1863. This is indeed a dark day for the Confederacy. Hundreds of our men are deserting and those who remain are discouraged and disheartened. To give up is but subjugation [enslavement]. To fight on is desolation [barrenness, bleakness].
>
> —*William Ross Stillwell, Headquarters Bryans Brigade.*
> *Longstreet Corp. McLaws Division. Chattanooga"*

- Clara Barton (founder of the Red Cross) said about women in the Civil War: "At the war's end, woman was at least fifty years in advance of the normal position which continued peace would have assigned her." How did the war open opportunities in nursing and government positions?

Disguised as a man, Frances Clalin served many months in the Missouri artillery and cavalry. (BPL)

- Write a short story or an essay about the women who disguised themselves to serve in the war.

Sample Chart

From *The Dispatch:*
Richmond, Virginia
January 29th 1863

"The Results of Extortion and Speculation." — The state of affairs brought about by the speculating and extortion practiced upon the public cannot be better illustrated than by the following grocery bill for one week for a small family, in which the prices before the war and those of the present are compared:

1860	1863
Bacon, 10 lbs. at 12 1/2 cents ... $1.25	Bacon, 10 lbs. at $1 .... $10.00
Flour, 30 lbs. at 5 cents 1.50	Flour, 30 lbs. at 12 1/2 cents 3.75
Sugar, 5 lbs. at 8 cents .... .40	Sugar, 5 lbs. at $1.15 .... 5.75
Coffee, 4 tbs. at 12 1/2 cents .... .50	Coffee, 4 lbs. at $5.00 .... 20.00
Tea (green), 1/2 lb. at $1 .... .50	Tea (green), 1/2 lb. at $16 .... 8.00
Lard, 4 lbs. at 12 1/2 cents .... .50	Lard, 4 lbs. at $1 .... 4.00
Butter, 3 lbs. at 25 cents .... .75	Butter, 3 lbs. at $1.75 .... 5.25
Meal, 1 pk. at 25 cents.................. .25	Meal, 1 pk. at $1 .... 1.00
Candles, 2 lbs. at 15 cents .... .30	Candles, 2 lbs. at $1.25 .... 2.50
Soap, 5 lbs. at 10 cents .... .50	Soap, 5 lbs. At $ 1.10 .... 5.50
Pepper and salt (about) .... .10	Pepper and salt (about).............. 2.50
Total............................ $6.55	**Total $68.25**

"So much we owe the speculators, who have stayed at home to prey upon the necessities of their fellow-citizens."

- Make a graph or draw a cartoon, based on the figures given above.
- Economic factors were among the chief causes of the Confederacy's defeat. Explain.

Young Soldiers

Portrait
of a boy
soldier.
(L.O.C.)

"Drummer" Taylor
of the 78th U. S.
Colored Infantry
(War Dept.)

Young Georgia Private
Edwin Jennison, killed in
the Seven Days Battles
at Malvern Hill (L.O.C.)

Bealeton, Va. Drum corps, 93rd New York Infantry, 1863.
(Timothy H. O'Sullivan, photographer, courtesy of L.O.C.)

• Gather some research on boy soldiers, then choose one of these photos
and write a short story or poem about it.

Suggested Further Reading

The books listed below are suggested readings in American literature, which tie in with *The Civil War: Researching American History Series*. The selections were made based on feedback from teachers and librarians currently using them in interdisciplinary classes for students in grades 4 to 12. Of course, there are many other historical novels that would be appropriate to tie in with the topics of slavery and the Civil War.

Charley Skedaddle, Patricia Beatty - M
Behind Rebel Lines, Seymour Reit - M
My Brother Sam is Dead, James L. Collier & Christopher Collier - M
Which Way Freedom, Joyce Hansen - M
Out from This Place, Joyce Hansen - M
Lincoln: A Photobiography, Russell Freedman - M
Abe Lincoln: Log Cabin to White House, Sterling A. North - M (biog.)
The Red Badge of Courage, Stephen Crane - M/HS
The Man Without a Country, Edward Everett Hale - HS
The Warrior Generals: Combat Leadership in the Civil War, T. B. Buell - HS
Slopes of War, Norah A. Perez - M
The Last Silk Dress, Ann Rinaldi - M
Perilous Road, William O. Steele - M
Rifles for Watie, Harold Keith - M/HS
Bigger, Patricia Calvert - M
The Andersonville Trial, Saul Levitt - HS (play)
Gone with the Wind, Margaret Mitchell - HS
The Autobiography of Miss Jane Pittman, Ernest J. Gaines - HS
Uncle Tom's Cabin, Harriet Beecher Stowe - HS
Classic Slave Narratives, Henry Louis Gates, Jr., editor - HS
Sojourner Truth: Ain't I A Woman, Sojourner Truth - HS
Harriet Tubman: Conductor on the Underground Railroad, Ann Petry - E/M
Brady, Jean Fritz - E/M
Nightjohn, Paulsen - M
Freedom Crossing, Margaret Goff Clark - M
A Girl Called Boy, Belinda Humerce - M
Jayhawker, Patricia Beatty - E/M
School for Pompey Walker, Michael Walker - E/M